CONTENTS

Author:
Andrew Robertshaw taught history before joining the
National Army Museum, Chelsea, in 1984. He is
currently responsible for the Museum's education services,
lifelong learning programme and special events as Head of
Learning Services. He is also an author, military historian
and battlefield guide. He lives in Surrey with his wife and
daughter.

Artist:
Mark Bergin studied at Eastbourne College of Art and
has specialised in historical reconstructions, aviation and
maritime subjects for over 20 years. He lives in Bexhill-
on-Sea with his wife and three children.

Additional artists: **Tony Townsend** and **Gerald Wood**

Series creator and designer: **David Salariya**
Editor: **Karen Barker Smith**
Assistant Editor: **Michael Ford**

With thanks to Mark and David at The Lanes Armoury.
www.thelanesarmoury.co.uk

Published in Great Britain in 2003 by
Book House, an imprint of
The Salariya Book Company Ltd
25 Marlborough Place, Brighton BN1 1UB

Please visit the Salariya Book Company at:
www.salariya.com
www.book-house.co.uk

ISBN 1 904194 78 8

A catalogue record for this book is available
from the British Library.

Printed and bound in Belgium.
Printed on paper from sustainable forests.

Photographic credits
t=top b=bottom c=centre l=left r=right

The Art Archive/ Dagli Orti: 9
The Art Archive/ Eileen Tweedy: 34tr
The Art Archive/ Musée des 2 Guerres Mondiales Paris/ Dagli
  Orti: 17
The Art Archive/ The Art Archive: 8b, 22b, 28b
The Art Archive/ The Imperial War Museum Photo archive
  IWM: 7t, 25t
Breslich & Foss: 19r, 20, 27, 28tr, 29l, 32r
Bridgeman Art Library: 15cr
IWM, The Trustees of the Imperial War Museum, London: 18b, 32l,
  33l, 35tr
Mark Bergin: 40c
Mary Evans Picture Library: 13tr
Mary Evans Picture Library/ Alexander Meledin: 27br
Mountain High maps/ copyright 1993 Digital Wisdom Inc: 6tl, 6b,
  8tl, 10tl, 22tl, 28tl, 34tl, 40tl
©Rene Burri/ Magnum Photos: 37b
©The Salariya Book Company: 1, 2-3, 4-5, 7br, 8c, 14b, 18tl, 19b,
  21t, 29b, 33tl, 37t, 42tr, 46-47, 48
Topham/Picturepoint: 36bl
©Werner Bischof/ Magnum Photos: 34b

BATTLE ZONES

Warfare in the 20th Century

Written by
Andrew Robertshaw

Illustrated by
Mark Bergin

BOOK HOUSE

Africa

THE BOER WAR, 1899-1902

Cork, cloth-covered helmet

British soldier from the Boer campaign

The Boer War began on 12th October, 1899, when the South African Republic (Transvaal) and the Orange Free State declared war on Great Britain to prevent the British Empire expanding further in Africa. The Boer republics lacked a regular army and were outnumbered by the forces of Britain and the Empire. It appeared that the Boer 'rabble of farmers' would be easily defeated. Instead, the war dragged on until 1902, costing the lives of 21,000 British soldiers, 7,000 Boer combatants and tens of thousands of civilians and became the first 'guerrilla' war of the 20th century.

BRITISH SOLDIERS

In 1899, most British soldiers were volunteers. Many soldiers had military experience in far-flung parts of the Empire and their equipment reflected this. They wore khaki-dyed cotton uniforms and cork, cloth-covered helmets to protect against the sun. Puttees – spiral bindings of cloth – supported their legs on long marches.

Khaki uniform

Puttees

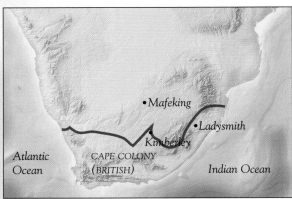

Southern region of Africa showing the besieged British garrisons

Although the British held out against sieges in the towns of Kimberley, Ladysmith and Mafeking, the war demonstrated their inadequacy against a mobile and well-armed enemy.

British troops in action in the Boer War

BOER SOLDIERS

The Boer military was based on the voluntary service of men aged between 16 and 60. The men provided their own horses, rations and equipment and used either their own rifle, or one provided by the Republic. The only 'regular' part of the force was the artillery, equipped with German and French guns and commanded by officers with European experience. The Boers were well armed, highly mobile and were fighting in a region they knew well.

A LONG WAY FROM HOME

The British Army was fighting more than 4,800 km from home and every bullet or tin of bully beef had to be sent by ship and then by rail or wagon. The army was forced to stay close to the railways, enabling the Boers to anticipate their routes. The Boers were able to blow up railway bridges and junctions to disrupt supplies.

BOER SURRENDER

In the summer of 1902 the last of the Boer 'bitter-enders' surrendered and a peace treaty granted the Boers internal self-government, as part of the Empire.

CONCENTRATION CAMPS

To prevent the Boers from getting supplies via their families it was decided to 'concentrate' the Boer women and children in camps. Although the camps were meant to offer protection and housing, bad administration and disease meant that more than 18,000 civilians died in these camps. More than 14,000 of the 21,000 British soldiers who died were killed by typhoid, cholera and dysentery.

NEW WEAPONS

The first true automatic machine guns were used in this conflict. They were able to fire up to 550 bullets a minute, but rifles caused the most casualties. The British Lee Enfield rifle (below) had a range of 2,560 metres but it was slower to load than the German Mauser used by the Boers.

British Lee Enfield rifle

RUSSO-JAPANESE WAR, 1904-5

Korea

It was not until the middle of the 19th century that Japan opened up to western ideas and technology. Central to that technology were modern warships. Japan rapidly developed a navy and within 40 years the nation went to war on its closest Asian rival, China. In the peace treaty that followed, Japan took control of Korea and a strip of Manchuria. Russia, France and Germany disagreed with this settlement and Manchuria was handed back to China. In return for this, China leased a naval base, later named Port Arthur, to Russia. The base was a direct threat to Japanese expansion in the region and in 1904 Japan siezed Port Arthur.

ATTACK ON PORT ARTHUR
The Japanese launched a surprise attack on the Russian fleet anchored in Port Arthur on 8th February. The fleet was badly damaged and never left harbour to confront Japanese Admiral Togo's ships. Lacking reinforcements in the Far East, the Russians decided to send a new fleet from the Baltic around Africa to fight the Japanese.

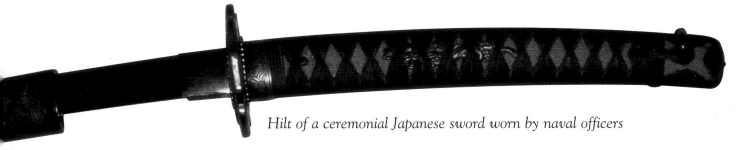

Hilt of a ceremonial Japanese sword worn by naval officers

Russian gunboat sinking off Port Arthur, May 1904, taken from a popular print of the time

JAPAN'S TACTICS
With the Russian fleet bottled up in harbour the Japanese landed thousands of men, besieging Port Arthur. They confronted the main Russian army near Mukden, a critical railway junction. The Japanese used many modern weapons, but frontal attacks against barbed wire and searchlights created thousands of casualties. The Russian garrison commander of Port Arthur, General Strossel, surrendered in January 1905, but by then the Japanese had lost two thirds of their troops.

Image from an April 1904 issue of French publication Le Petit Journal *showing the Russian ship* Petropavlovsk *being torpedoed by the Japanese*

RUSSIAN DEFEAT

When Port Arthur surrendered the rest of the Russian fleet was at Madagascar, on the east coast of Africa. They had sailed over 12,000 km in less than two months. Russian Admiral Rozhdestvensky ordered his ships to head for Vladivostok and safety but the fleet was detected by the Japanese Navy on 29th May, 1905. The following battle, the first between fleets of ironclads, was a disaster for the Russians. Admiral Rozhdestvensky was wounded and eventually taken prisoner. Admiral Togo handled his fleet of modern ships well – most of the Russian ships were sunk and many more were captured.

Europe

THE GREAT WAR, 1914-18

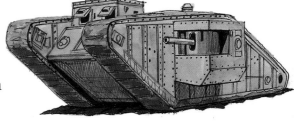

The heir to the Austro-Hungarian throne, Archduke Ferdinand, was assassinated in Bosnia in June 1914. The Austro-Hungarians blamed Serbia and demanded that the country be punished, but the Serbs, backed by Russia, refused to back down. Germany backed Austria, France supported Russia and the final steps to war began. The Germans planned an initial attack on France followed by a defeat of Russia. Known as the 'Schlieffen Plan', this involved an attack through Belgium, which Britain had agreed to defend. In 1915, Turkey and Italy sided with Germany and by this time fighting was also taking place in Africa, China and the Middle East. The United States became involved in 1917 when German submarines threatened the freedom of the seas and appeared to back a Mexican invasion of the USA.

FIRST TANKS
Tanks were developed as a means of crossing trenches, crushing barbed wire and destroying gun placements. They were first used in September 1916 during the Battle of the Somme. Although initially successful, these first vehicles proved to be slow and unreliable and it wasn't until the end of 1917 that they were used in large numbers.

BRITISH ARMY
The British army of 1914 was tiny compared to the conscript armies of France and Germany. Its soldiers were highly professional and well equipped for a brief mobile war.

Khaki uniform

Equipment carried in cotton webbing bags

British infantryman

FRENCH ARMY
Most European armies had adopted a camouflaged uniform by this time, but the French army wore blue, a throwback to the Napoleonic Wars in the 1870s.

Rifle with bayonet

Blue uniform

French soldier

GERMAN ARMY
In August 1914 conscripted German troops were sent west on thousands of trains. Long columns of advancing troops marched many kilometres through France but Paris did not fall. The Germans were forced to dig in to hold the ground that they had captured and the scene was set for trench warfare.

Pickelhaube helmet

German soldier

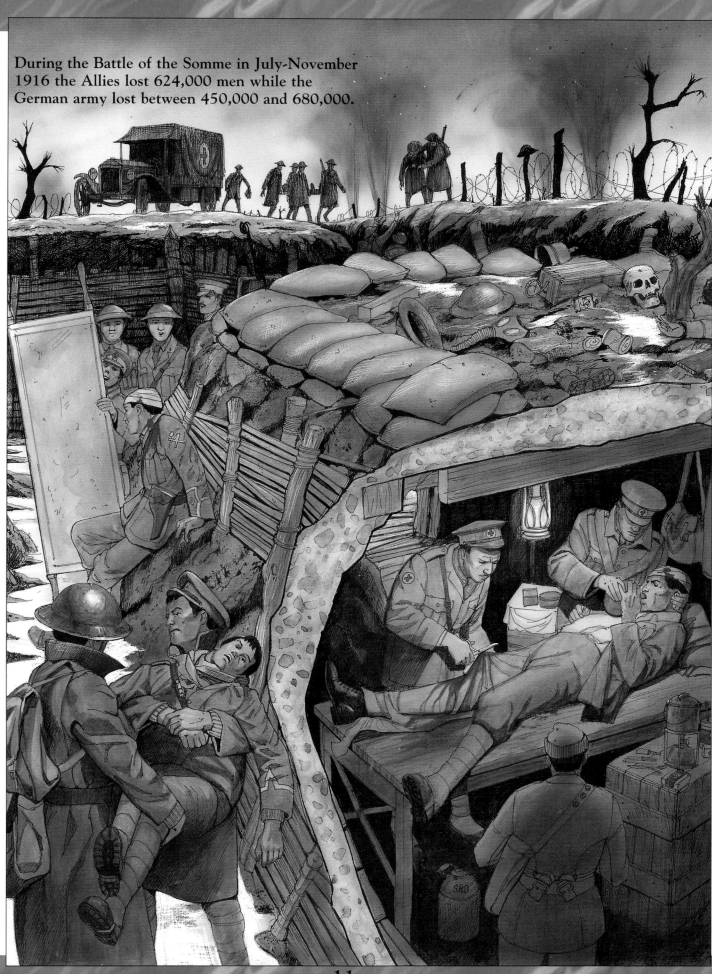

During the Battle of the Somme in July-November 1916 the Allies lost 624,000 men while the German army lost between 450,000 and 680,000.

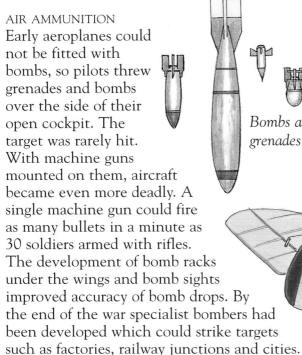

AIR AMMUNITION

Early aeroplanes could not be fitted with bombs, so pilots threw grenades and bombs over the side of their open cockpit. The target was rarely hit. With machine guns mounted on them, aircraft became even more deadly. A single machine gun could fire as many bullets in a minute as 30 soldiers armed with rifles. The development of bomb racks under the wings and bomb sights improved accuracy of bomb drops. By the end of the war specialist bombers had been developed which could strike targets such as factories, railway junctions and cities.

Bombs and grenades

The British Bristol Fighter (below) had a two-man crew – the pilot and an observer or gunner.

Bristol Fighter

AIR WARFARE

The first powered flight, by the Wright brothers in North Carolina, USA, was in December 1903. Eleven years later all the nations involved in the Great War had air forces consisting of both airships and aeroplanes. Early in the war aeroplanes took over the task of reconnaissance. It was the British Royal Flying Corps (RFC) that first detected German troops and later saw that the Germans would not encircle Paris. By the end of the conflict planes had bombed London, enabled the battlefield to be mapped by means of photography and had made 'aces' of pilots who engaged in dogfights. Early aircraft were unarmed and pilots might wave to each other rather than fight. Later pilots carried pistols and rifles and others dropped grenades and darts onto troops on the ground. With the fitting of machine guns, pilots could aim their aircraft at a target and shoot it down. If a pilot was shot down he had few options for escape. Parachutes were heavy and some air forces banned them altogether!

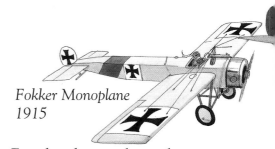

Fokker Monoplane 1915

Fitted with a single machine gun, this aircraft shot down hundreds of Allied planes during the winter of 1915-1916.

AERIAL WARFARE

Sometimes it was the skill of an individual pilot that made him an 'ace', but increasingly pilots fought in formation, giving mutual support and protection. This was vital so the slower reconnaissance planes could carry out observation and photography duties without being shot down by the faster 'scouts'.

FOKKER TRIPLANE

Although small and slow, the Fokker Triplane (below) was perhaps the most agile aircraft of the war. German aircraft frequently sported bright colours to identify units and individual planes.

Fokker Triplane 1917

THE RED BARON

Baron Manfred Freiherr von Richthofen (above) flew an all-red plane and was the best pilot ace of the war with 80 'kills'. Richthofen himself was shot down in April 1918.

This symbol (left) was carried on the SPAD aircraft of Captain Edward V. Rickenbacker of the United States Air Service – the best US pilot ace of the war. Some high scoring pilots, including 'Billy' Bishop of the RFC and Georges Guynemer of the French Air Force, became famous.

SPAD 13 1917

Sopwith Camel 1918

Albatross DVa 1917

Bristol BE2c 1914

This was an observation plane used by the RFC.

The SPAD was a French fighter also used by the Americans, Belgians and British.

The most successful Allied scout of the war, Sopwith Camels shot down nearly 1,300 enemy planes.

The German Albatross had a form of camouflage to break up its outline and a powerful engine.

BIG GUNS, BIG SHELLS

A 305-mm shell weighing 386 kg could travel nearly 17 km. This projectile could punch a hole through a ship and only very thick steel armour could resist the force of such a shell. By 1913, ships like the *HMS Queen Elizabeth*, a super-Dreadnought, mounted 381-mm guns.

Metal shells with explosive tips and filled with metal balls

FIRST CLASH OF THE DREADNOUGHTS

On 31st May, 1916, the Royal Navy and the German Imperial fleet clashed in the North Sea at the Battle of Jutland. The German fleet was able to sink a number of the smaller British battle cruisers but had a large number of vessels damaged and was forced to withdraw. German weapons proved to be more accurate than their opponents' and did more damage due to better shells. The German High Seas Fleet never went into action again in the war – their next voyage was to surrender in November 1918.

HMS Dreadnought

WAR AT SEA

Royal Navy officer's dress uniform at the time of the Great War

In October 1906 the Royal Navy began trials of a ship that revolutionised naval warfare, *HMS Dreadnought*. Armed with ten 305-mm guns and with a top speed of 23 knots (42.6 kph) it looked as if just one of these new 'dreadnoughts' could defeat a fleet of older vessels. Every nation in the world had to build comparable ships to stand any hope of competing with the Royal Navy. By 1914 Britain had 29 completed dreadnoughts and 16 being built, whilst Germany had 21 completed and six under construction.

BRITISH NAVAL UNIFORM

The dress uniform of a British naval officer (left) included a dark blue double-breasted swallow-tailed coat with gold buttons, lace and epaulettes, and a white gold-edged slashed-flap on the sleeve with rings of lace showing rank.

British 'E' Class submarine

SUBMARINES

Submarines were experimented with as far back as the Napoleonic Wars (1793-1815) but their use in the Great War made them a threat to the world's navies and merchant fleets. The submarines were driven by electricity and used torpedoes as their main weapon. By 1914 the Royal Navy had 37 submarines and the French 36. Fortunately for the Allies, Germany was slow at developing its submarine fleet and had only 27 at the outbreak of war. However, one German submarine sank three British cruisers on 22nd September, 1914.

LUSITANIA, 1915

By the second year of the war the Allies' naval blockade of German shipping was highly effective and the German navy was keen to enforce its own blockade of Allied goods. In May 1915 the liner *Lusitania* sailed from New York. Off the Irish coast, the vessel was hit by a torpedo fired from a German U20 submarine. *Lusitania* sank quickly, killing 1,195 of the 1,959 passengers, including 123 American citizens. The United States, a neutral nation, warned the Germans that any future act of aggression would be a declaration of war. Two years later the declaration of unrestricted submarine warfare by the Germans contributed to the decision by the US to join the Allies. Despite an exploration of the wreck, it is unclear to this day whether the *Lusitania* was carrying munitions for the British war industry.

Contemporary painting of the sinking of the Lusitania

German U31 submarine

Conning tower

Gun mounted on deck

Mine-laying submarine (not to scale with the U31)

TORPEDOES, GUNS AND MINES

Torpedoes were the main weapons of submarines, but a gun could also be mounted on the deck in front of the conning tower when the submarine was on the surface. This gun could sink unarmoured vessels, saving the torpedoes for bigger prey. Some specialist submarines carried mines that could be laid in harbours or sea lanes where enemy vessels were bound to hit them.

THE EASTERN FRONT

The German war plan did not anticipate the rapid mobilisation of the Russian armies, made up of one and a half million men. When the Russians marched into East Prussia the Germans found themselves outnumbered. In danger of encirclement the Germans attacked at Tannenberg and between 26th-30th August, 1914, inflicted 250,000 casualties on the Russian forces. Two weeks later a second Russian defeat occurred at the Battle of the Masurian Lakes.

With a massive population but under-developed industry, Russia was able to replace artillery and other weapons with manpower. Russian troops were badly armed – sometimes having to share rifles – badly fed and had little chance of leave. Still they fought for 'Mother Russia' and the Tsar. The war bogged down and a system of trenches was established. Although both sides were able to make advances that would have been monumental on the Western Front, these meant little in the vast open spaces of Russia.

Cossack in the Russian cavalry

COSSACKS
The wide-open spaces of the Eastern Front meant that cavalry could be used to some effect although not against entrenched positions. The Cossacks were the most skilled and feared of the Russian cavalrymen (above).

WINTER FIGHTING
Both sides dug trenches for protection. However, the climate and shortage of artillery meant that dugouts, built deep underground on the Western Front, were constructed more like huts with stoves. The men had to be issued with special clothing, but the ill-equipped Russian soldiers frequently had to manage with little more than vodka to keep them going.

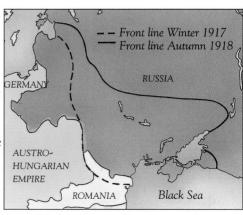

Map of the Eastern Front 1917-1918

RUSSIAN PATRIOTISM

Despite the patriotic appeal of this poster (right), a request to fund the war, Russian society was unable to support a major conflict as it had relatively little industry, an inadequate railway system and a poor peasantry who did little more than survive. A revolution in 1905 after the Russo-Japanese war had shown that many sections of society wanted reform but by 1917 it was too late.

Russian patriotic poster appealing for funds for the war effort

THE TSAR

In March 1917, with his forces in disarray, Tsar Nicholas II abdicated. The Bolsheviks (see below) moved the royal family (above), including Empress Alexandra and five children, to Siberia. From there they were sent to Ekaterinburg in the Urals and were executed on 17th July, 1918.

BRUSILOV OFFENSIVE

In the summer of 1916 a brilliant Russian General Brusilov led a victorious offensive, inflicting heavy losses on the Austrians. The Germans feared that the whole Eastern Front would collapse but with Russian losses running into the millions (one million in 1916 alone) the Russian troops began to lose heart and victory appeared impossible. Increasingly troops refused to attack or simply deserted. Even before the Bolshevik revolution the Russian army had split into political factions and was melting away.

Portrait of Vladimir Lenin

LENIN

In April 1917 the Germans sent Vladimir Ilich Ulyanov Lenin (left), a Marxist, to the Russian capital, Petrograd (St Petersburg) as a means of causing a revolution and undermining the Russian war effort. In November, following a period of unrest in the city, Lenin and his Bolshevik party took control. They agreed a harsh peace treaty with Germany in March 1918 and Russia was out of the war. Conflict between Red (Communist) and White (Tsarist) forces continued.

GERMAN SPRING OFFENSIVE, 1918

With Russia out of the war, Germany turned west to defeat the Allies, who in turn were being reinforced by the United States (the American Expeditionary Force). One quarter of the German force was reclassified as attack divisions for this new offensive, while the remainder became trench divisions designed to hold ground. The attack divisions received new and better weapons, training and rations. The battle began on 21st March, 1918 and, with a bombardment of both gas and shells combined with dense fog, the German attack was an outstanding success. The Germans captured thousands of British prisoners and hundreds of guns in the initial stages of the offensive. The British commander, Field Marshal Sir Douglas Haig, issued an order stating that the army had its "back to the wall". Within days the offensive slowed. The Germans were unable to provide their troops with supplies because of the broken ground caused by previous fighting and were demoralised by the abundance of Allied rations and weapons they found as they advanced.

US trench 'knuckle' knife, 1918, used in hand-to-hand fighting

IN THE TRENCHES

For much of the time trench warfare was a matter of routine – no matter which side of no man's land a soldier was on. Soldiers spent about a week in the front line, working at night to dig trenches or build barbed-wire defences. After a period in the trenches time was spent in reserve, resting, training or marching to a new location. Major attacks were rare and few soldiers 'hopped the bags', or attacked, more than a couple of times a year.

British raiding party manoeuvring along a trench

German Storm Trooper

STORM TROOPERS

In the forefront of a German attack or counter-attack were the *Stosstruppen* (Storm Troopers). These were younger, better fed and better armed than the rest of the army. They were formed into specialist units for raids or capturing positions. Although they had a good reputation there was danger in relying on 'elite' troops. Their units inevitably received the largest number of casualties and once these men had gone the remaining soldiers could do little more than hold their position.

AMERICAN SOLDIERS

The trenches were a new experience for American soldiers. They wore American uniforms but were issued with British-style helmets and respirators, drove French-made tanks and fired French guns. What they lacked in experience was made up for in enthusiasm. The 'Dough Boys' (so-called due to the shape of their packs) lacked the 'war weariness' of the other Allies.

A ceremonial German Pickelhaube helmet made with leather and gilded brass (below)

Spike intended to create the image of a highly aggressive military force

British-style helmet

Pack

Re-creation of an American soldier

THE ARMISTICE

The Allies counter-offensive began in August, near Amiens. In the last 100 days the war left the trenches and by the end of the autumn the German army had been pushed back to where they had begun in 1914. At 11.00 am on 11th November, 1918, the Armistice was signed and the Great War ended.

THE GREAT WAR OUTSIDE EUROPE

ANZACS

The Australian and New Zealand Army Corps (ANZACS) is most famous for its role in the Gallipoli landings and later battles. Here these tough soldiers demonstrated their fighting abilities.

Slouch hat for hot climates

Re-creation of a Private of the Australian Imperial Force

Although notoriously resistant to discipline, the ANZACS won the admiration of their commanders and opponents at Gallipoli and later when they were transferred to the Western Front.

Although the war began in Europe conflict spilled into many corners of the world. The Allies wished to seize Germany's overseas empire and wanted to break the stalemate on the Western Front by finding alternative ways to advance. When Turkey sided with Germany war in the Middle East became inevitable. Turkey posed a threat to the Suez Canal and controlled the shipping route from the Mediterranean to the Black Sea.

Although these campaigns became known as the 'Side Shows' they involved large numbers of troops and casualties. However, unlike the Western Front, it was disease that caused the most deaths, not enemy action.

White cloth to identify infantry

GALLIPOLI

When Turkey entered the war in November 1914 British and French fleets planned to force their way through the sea route to Constantinople (now known as Istanbul). This failed disastrously and an alternative plan to land on the Gallipoli peninsula was formed. The initial landings, in April 1915, were followed by others further up the peninsula by troops including the ANZACS, French, Indians and Gurkhas. The offensive rapidly became a stalemate and both sides dug into trenches just like the Western Front. Unable to advance, and after the loss of 36,000 lives, the Allies evacuated the peninsula in January 1916.

Jambiya horn-hilt dagger and sheath, with inlaid silver, of the sort worn by T.E. Lawrence

T.E. LAWRENCE

Thomas Edward Lawrence was a British historian with a knowledge of Arabic culture and language who volunteered in Cairo at the start of the war. In 1916 he joined the forces of Sheik Feisel al Husayn in the British-backed revolt against Turkish rule. He led Arab forces in a successful guerrilla campaign that distracted the Turkish army while the British began successful campaigns against Turkish-controlled Palestine and Syria. His fame as an Arab leader led to him becoming known as 'Lawrence of Arabia'.

GREAT ARAB REVOLT

When Turkey joined the Central Powers in late 1914 the Arab people saw an opportunity to free themselves from Turkish oppression and in 1916 they began the Great Arab Revolt. By the end of the war they had, with Allied assistance, captured all of Jordan, much of Syria and most of the Arabian peninsula.

GERMANY'S EMPIRE

Part of Germany's Empire, along with Cameroon, Togoland and German South West Africa, was the colony of German East Africa. On 3rd November, 1914, an invasion force of 30,000 British and Indian troops landed at Tanga Bay. Their goal was to defeat German Lieutenant Colonel Paul von Lettow-Vorbeck and his 4,000 men. By the end of the day the invasion force had been defeated and fled. This was the beginning of an epic resistance that did not end until two days after the Armistice had been signed. The only outside assistance von Lettow-Vorbeck received was from the crew of a German cruiser who brought him some naval guns for which he improvised land carriages.

T.E. Lawrence, known as 'Lawrence of Arabia'

SECOND WORLD WAR, 1939-45

Europe

The Second World War began on 1st September, 1939, when Nazi Germany invaded Poland. This initial conflict saw a speed of advance that had never been encountered before. The Germans called this style of warfare 'blitzkrieg' (lightning war). Using mechanised units with heavy tanks combined with air supremacy, the Nazi forces crushed the Polish army and air force. Warsaw, the Polish capital, surrendered on 27th September. Although France and Britain declared war on Nazi Germany they could do little to aid Poland. There was no further fighting in Europe until the spring of 1940.

PANZERS

The German armoured units (Panzers) used tanks in an innovative way. Tanks were massed together to ensure that they outnumbered opponents. They were followed by motorised transport for the infantry and support troops. Artillery was largely replaced by air attack. The plan was to use these units to break through enemy lines and to keep going, disrupting supplies and destroying the ability to control troops.

German Panzer tanks

German Führer Adolf Hitler surveying his troops in Poland

THE FALL OF FRANCE

In the period between the surrender of Poland and spring 1940, Britain and France faced Nazi Germany. The French were certain that the concrete fortifications of the Maginot line along the German border would halt any attack. However, on 10th May, 1940, Nazi forces struck at France, Belgium and Holland. Using their blitzkrieg tactics the attack ignored the Maginot line, cut through the enemy and reached the Channel coast. Italy had signed a 'Pact of Steel' with Nazi Germany in 1939 and declared war on Britain and France when the Nazis invaded France.

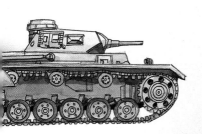

German Stuka dive bombers

DUNKIRK

Between 27th May and 4th June nearly 340,000 Allied soldiers were evacuated from the beaches near Dunkirk. Belgium and Holland surrendered and Paris fell. On 22nd June the French signed an armistice with Nazi Germany. The war had lasted six weeks. With Europe occupied it looked as if Britain was now fighting alone and would not hold out for long. Hitler visited his troops rehearsing the invasion of Britain, 'Operation Sea Lion', and he watched the white cliffs of Dover through binoculars.

STUKAS

Aircraft were a vital part of the blitzkrieg. The Stuka (Junkers 87), a specialist dive bomber, had sirens fastened to its wings so that the sound would add terror to the effect of the bombs.

HAWKER HURRICANES

The Hawker Hurricane provided the bulk of the RAF fighters during the battle. Steady and robust, the Hurricane was a match for its German fighter opponent, the Bf 109E, as long as the German plane did not have an altitude advantage. The Hurricane's eight machine guns provided the fighter with a total of about 15 seconds firing time. Both types of aircraft flew in a team of two – a leader and 'wing man' to give mutual protection.

Spitfire

Messerschmitt Bf 109E, a German fighter

SUPERMARINE SPITFIRE

The Supermarine Spitfire was faster and more manoeuvrable than the Hurricane. During battle the superiority of the Spitfire's performance meant that if possible they engaged the German fighters while the Hurricanes attacked the bombers. Its elegant lines and distinctive appearance made the Spitfire a symbol of the Battle of Britain.

THE BATTLE OF BRITAIN

By the summer of 1940 the Luftwaffe (German Air Force) had defeated every opponent they had faced. Now only the British Royal Air Force (RAF) stood between them and their ability to protect a Nazi invasion fleet, which was preparing to invade Britain. If the Luftwaffe could destroy the RAF it looked as if the fall of Britain would be inevitable. Following Dunkirk the RAF faced increasing attacks and throughout the late summer and autumn of 1940 British Hurricanes and Spitfires took on waves of bombers and fighters in the air over southern England. Losses were heavy on both sides, but whereas every British pilot who survived being shot down over England could be expected to return to action, all Luftwaffe crew became prisoners.

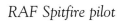

RAF Spitfire pilot

Aerial view of a German bomber over London

FIGHTERS AND BOMBERS

Despite the fire power of the German fighter, the Messerschmitt Bf 109E could not turn as well as RAF fighters. Also, by the time the German planes had flown from occupied France they could not stay in the air for long over Britain. Many ran out of fuel on their return journey. The Heinkel He 111 was one of the main German bombers used in the battle.

German fighter pilot

German bomber crew member

THE BLITZ

On the night of 24th August, 1940, German bombers attacked London and the RAF retaliated with a raid on Berlin. Hitler responded by ordering further attacks, lasting from 7th September to 5th October, known as the Blitz. Thousands of civilians were killed and London was extensively damaged, but the Luftwaffe were no longer attacking RAF airfields. Civilian morale was shaken, but the use of air-raid shelters, including the underground rail system, gave confidence.

Although more than 1,000 men (one third of the RAF crew who took part in the battles) were lost, the Luftwaffe failed to defeat them. The use of the new invention, radar, which could detect bombers before they could be seen, together with skilful tactics, meant that German losses always exceeded British. Hitler's Operation Sea Lion was repeatedly postponed and finally cancelled in February 1941.

RUSSIAN FRONT, 1941-45

Female Soviet soldier

*A*lthough Hitler had signed a pact with Soviet leader Stalin and had shared some Polish territory with the USSR (Union of Soviet Socialist Republics) in 1940, he had no peaceful intentions towards this country. On 22nd June, 1941, without a declaration of war, Hitler launched 'Operation Barbarossa' using 160 divisions. Although the blitzkrieg was as effective as usual and the number of prisoners taken was impressive, the Soviets bought time by using the vast expanses of space in their country. They fell back and applied a 'scorched earth' policy, leaving nothing but wasteland in their wake. The further they withdrew the more extended the Nazi supply lines became. By the autumn Nazi forces were at the gates of principal cities including Moscow, Leningrad (present-day St. Petersburg) and Stalingrad (present-day Volgograd).

FEMALE COMBATANTS
Unlike other Allied forces, Soviet women served in the front line as soldiers, snipers, tank crew and fighter pilots.

SOVIET TANKS
Tanks such as the T34 and SU-12 (armed with a 122-mm gun) were the products of a Soviet industry that could make farming and heavy engineering equipment. They were robust, mounted a heavier gun than their opposition and were diesel-fuelled, which meant they were less likely to burn if a tank was damaged in battle.

GERMAN ADVANCE
German tanks improved in size and effectiveness but most remained relatively thinly armoured and mounted small-calibre guns. The Panther had sloped armour and a 75-mm calibre weapon. Although the Nazi advance covered about 900 km by Christmas 1941, the Russian policy of removing industry deprived them of victory. They had to endure the worst winter on record while besieging a series of major cities.

Soviet T34 tank

German Panther tank

PPSh-41
submachine gun

SIEGE OF STALINGRAD

The Nazi siege of Stalingrad, the city named after the Soviet leader Joseph Stalin, became an epic struggle. In September 1942, following the spring thaw, the Nazi army got to the outskirts of the city and the River Volga. General von Paulus and his Sixth Army of 300,000 men failed to clear out the defenders who fought for every building. Finally, the Soviet forces surrounded von Paulus and in January 1943 he and his surviving troops were taken prisoner.

Russian advances in 1944

THE ROAD TO BERLIN

With their own troop reinforcements and with weapons, vehicles and equipment from the USA and Britain, the Soviets began an advance. By April 1945 they were at the gates of Berlin and had taken Poland, the Baltic States, Yugoslavia, Hungary, Romania, Bulgaria and Austria.

Despite fanatical resistance from the Nazis, Marshal Zhukov, who commanded the Soviet's central army groups, finally secured Berlin on 2nd May, 1945, with heavy loss of life. Hitler had already committed suicide on 30th April and the war in Europe was over.

Soviet tanks rolling into Berlin, 1945

Re-creation of a
Soviet soldier

SOVIET SOLDIER

Soviet soldiers were armed with sound and simple weapons such as the PPSh-41 submachine gun. Soviet commanders had an almost unlimited number of conscripted soldiers at their disposal and could afford casualties. The Nazis, fighting on two fronts from June 1944, could not.

WAR IN THE PACIFIC

Japan and South East Asia

Although it was clear that tension between Imperial Japan, the USA and European governments was growing, the first Japanese strike on Pearl Harbor, Hawaii, in December 1941 was a total surprise. Within a few months, the Japanese had invaded and overrun virtually all of the countries of South East Asia and the Pacific. They were marching on India, through Burma and looked ready to attack Australia. The tide turned for the Allies in June 1942 when, at the Island of Midway in the Pacific, a Japanese invasion force was smashed by American air attack alone. Then began the slow and difficult task of pushing the Japanese back to the mainland. It would take over three years.

JAPANESE SOLDIERS
In 1941, Japanese soldiers underwent harsh training. Many had experience of fighting during the long conflict against China. The Japanese Emperor had the status of a god and every Japanese soldier thought it was an honour to die in battle. Being taken prisoner was the ultimate disgrace to both a soldier and his family.

Re-creation of a Japanese soldier in winter uniform in the Second World War

PEARL HARBOR
The attack on the United States Pacific fleet at Pearl Harbor on 7th December, 1941, was a crushing blow, described by President Roosevelt as a day "that will live in infamy". The number of casualties and ships and aircraft lost made the Americans resolute to revenge the attack. The USA declared war on both Japan and Nazi Germany. Final victory would involve defeating both powers.

Thompson submachine gun, known as a 'Tommy gun'

Fibre-lined helmet

Identity tags, known as 'dog tags'

US MARINES

The United States Marines used specially designed landing craft and tracked vehicles to get through the surf and onto the beaches of the Japanese-held islands. Once ashore, field craft and teamwork allowed the Marines to break through the enemy defences. Japanese soldiers were masters of camouflage. Time after time they emerged behind groups of advancing Americans or made terrifying banzai charges, facing certain death rather than becoming prisoners.

AIR POWER

Throughout the Pacific campaign control of the air was vital. The Allied Lockheed P-38 Lightning was responsible for destroying more enemy aircraft in the Pacific than any other fighter. The Mitsubishi A6M, or 'Zero', was Japan's most important fighter and flew from shore bases and aircraft carriers.

Lockheed P-38 Lightning

Mitsubishi A6M

KAMIKAZE PILOTS

The Japanese tried a new suicide tactic, the kamikaze (divine wind) attack. Japanese pilots deliberately crashed their planes onto Allied vessels, sacrificing their life to sink an enemy ship.

Knife of a Second World War kamikaze pilot

THE ATOMIC BOMB

By August 1945 plans were well advanced for an Allied landing on Japan. However, it was decided to use a new weapon, the atomic bomb. The first hit Hiroshima on 6th August killing as many as 150,000 people. Three days later, another atomic bomb destroyed Nagasaki. Unconditional surrender by Japanese Emperor Hirohito followed on 14th August. The war in the Pacific was over.

Re-creation of a United States Marine in the lightweight cotton uniform suitable for fighting in hot climates

BATTLE OF THE ATLANTIC

With mainland Europe under occupation, the Atlantic Ocean was a lifeline for Britain. The country relied on the hundreds of merchant ships bringing vital food and weapons to ports such as Liverpool and Southampton. Despite British government appeals to the public to grow more food, transforming parks and gardens into allotments, most supplies had to be carried across the Atlantic by the British Merchant Navy. The German navy used ships and U-boats (submarines) to attack merchant ships, hoping to starve Britain out of the war.

Allied aircraft fitted with radar (radio detecting and ranging) equipment were a vital weapon against the U-boats

HEAVY WEATHER

In stormy conditions U-boats could avoid the worst of the wind and waves by submerging. On the surface they had the advantage of seeing enemy vessels. They could use squalls and spray to approach to torpedo firing range undetected. The discomfort was worth it if a torpedo found its target.

U-boat on the surface during a gale

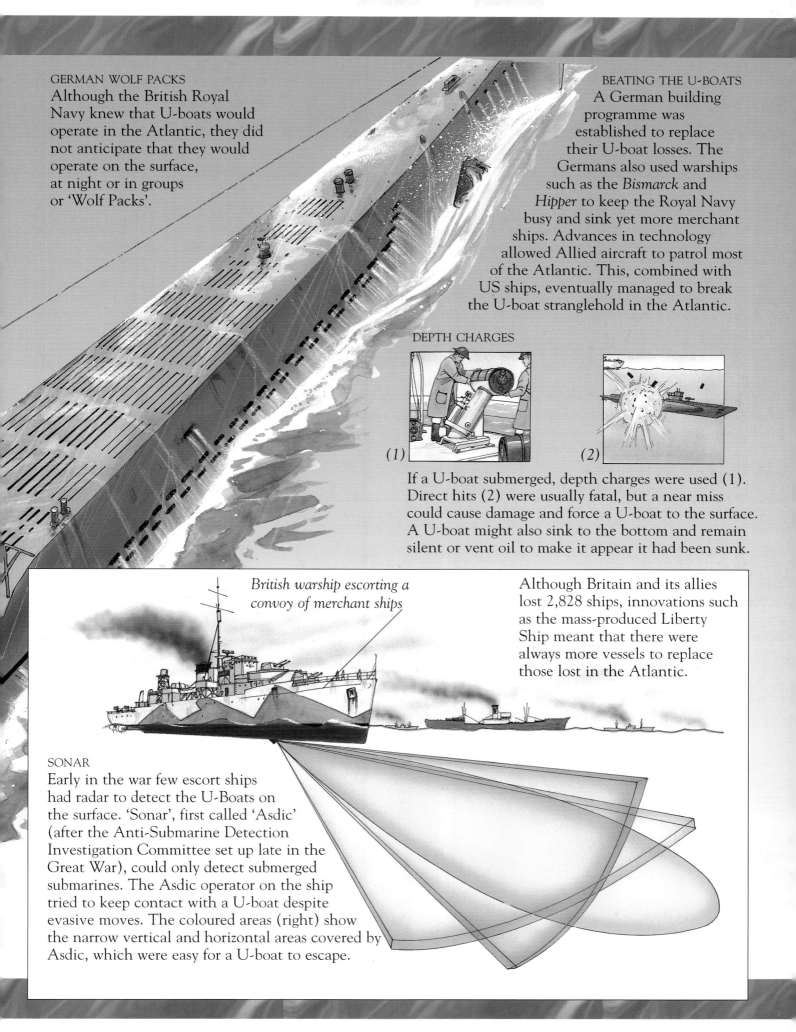

GERMAN WOLF PACKS

Although the British Royal Navy knew that U-boats would operate in the Atlantic, they did not anticipate that they would operate on the surface, at night or in groups or 'Wolf Packs'.

BEATING THE U-BOATS

A German building programme was established to replace their U-boat losses. The Germans also used warships such as the *Bismarck* and *Hipper* to keep the Royal Navy busy and sink yet more merchant ships. Advances in technology allowed Allied aircraft to patrol most of the Atlantic. This, combined with US ships, eventually managed to break the U-boat stranglehold in the Atlantic.

DEPTH CHARGES

(1)   *(2)*

If a U-boat submerged, depth charges were used (1). Direct hits (2) were usually fatal, but a near miss could cause damage and force a U-boat to the surface. A U-boat might also sink to the bottom and remain silent or vent oil to make it appear it had been sunk.

British warship escorting a convoy of merchant ships

Although Britain and its allies lost 2,828 ships, innovations such as the mass-produced Liberty Ship meant that there were always more vessels to replace those lost in the Atlantic.

SONAR

Early in the war few escort ships had radar to detect the U-Boats on the surface. 'Sonar', first called 'Asdic' (after the Anti-Submarine Detection Investigation Committee set up late in the Great War), could only detect submerged submarines. The Asdic operator on the ship tried to keep contact with a U-boat despite evasive moves. The coloured areas (right) show the narrow vertical and horizontal areas covered by Asdic, which were easy for a U-boat to escape.

EUROPE, 1944-45

Following Pearl Harbor, American troops poured into Britain. From 1942 there were plans to 'open a second front', the first being the Russian front. In 1943, after the Nazis were defeated in Africa, the Allies landed in Sicily and Italy and gradually advanced to capture Rome in June 1944.

Hitler anticipated an Allied invasion and constructed a line of defences down the coast of occupied Europe nicknamed the 'Atlantic Wall'. This consisted of bunkers, pill boxes (concrete bunkers and gun positions), mine fields and sea defences. Behind these defences were tanks and mobile units. The defences were strongest where the Channel was narrowest, around Calais and the main harbours. As a result the Allies decided to attack in Normandy, taking floating 'Mulberry harbours' with them.

Camouflage on helmet

Soldiers taking part in the D Day invasion had a French guidebook and money in their kit

Lee Enfield No.4 rifle

Shovel

Re-creation of a British soldier and equipment

British paratroopers synchronising watches before going into action

It was not until June 1944 that the Allied plans for 'Operation Overlord' were finally ready. The Allies used everything at their disposal by launching the biggest amphibious operation in history. This involved dropping thousands of paratroops (parachute troops) behind the defenders of Hitler's 'Atlantic Wall'. The day for the invasion was code-named D Day.

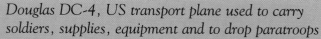

Douglas DC-4, US transport plane used to carry soldiers, supplies, equipment and to drop paratroops

Service medal awarded to British soldiers serving in the Second World War

D DAY, 6TH JUNE 1944

The first troops to land on D Day were British parachute and glider troops who landed just before midnight on 5th June. During the day that followed Allied troops, commanded by General Dwight Eisenhower, landed on five invasion beaches and by the evening they were ashore to stay. All Allied aircraft taking part in the operation were painted with black and white 'invasion stripes' to prevent them being shot down by their own troops.

General Patton was given command of the First United States Army Group (FUSAG) – a group of decoy tents, vehicles and landing craft stationed on the English coast facing Calais. This deception convinced Hitler that the Normandy landings were a diversion. By August 1944 the Allies were able to break out of the Normandy 'bridgehead' and by Christmas France, Belgium and southern Holland had been 'liberated'. On 4th May, 1945, the Nazi army in the west surrendered and 8th May, 1945, was declared VE – Victory in Europe – Day.

Allied Sherman tanks

ALLIED LANDINGS

Sherman tanks (above) were used by the US, Canadian and British forces in the attack. Fighting in the Normandy 'Bocage' (densely hedged fields, restricting movement and visibility) was fierce but Allied air supremacy and superior numbers gradually helped to expand their landings.

KOREA, 1950-53

Korea

During the Second World War Korea was occupied by Japan. At the end of the conflict, the Soviets coming from the north and the Americans landing in the south divided the country between them. The border was agreed as the 38th Parallel, chosen simply because it was a convenient line on a map. Both sides installed their own 'puppet' regime and as relations between the Western powers and the Soviet Union worsened at the start of the 'Cold War' (see pages 36-37) so did that between North and South Korea. On 25th June, 1950, the Soviet-trained Korean People's Army attacked the South. The South Korean army collapsed, abandoning Seoul, the capital. On the same day the United Nations (UN) passed a resolution condemning North Korea and calling for a withdrawal. Within days the first UN troops landed to resist the North Korean advance.

Propaganda poster issued by the UN, showing North Korean soldiers leading Korea into Communist slavery

South Korean soldiers at Kaesong, just below the 38th Parallel

UN INVOLVEMENT

UN forces, mostly from the United States, were driven back to the far south east around the port of Pusan. This was followed by a UN amphibious landing at Inchon, north west of Seoul, and a drive north that led to the involvement of Chinese communist 'volunteers' from the People's Republic of China. Despite a threat by the UN to use atomic weapons, they were again pushed south during the winter of 1951. The communists took thousands of UN prisoners of war (POWs), whose treatment was particularly harsh.

The first truce talks between North and South Korea were held in 1951, at Kaesong (left). In 1953 Kaesong was incorporated into North Korea.

MASH UNITS

In previous wars, although it was understood that speed was vital in treating the wounded, evacuation by stretcher and ambulance took time. Often patients died or their condition worsened during this journey. The development of helicopters at the end of the Second World War allowed casualties to be airlifted from the battlefield straight to the medical units. The Mobile Army Surgical Hospitals (MASH) came into being. Thousands of UN personnel and Koreans owed their lives to these units during the three years of the war.

MASH unit in action in Korea

Sabre F-86

JET AIRCRAFT

For the first time in conflict both sides were operating jet aircraft. The American Sabre (left) proved to be a fast and effective fighter against its Soviet-built opponents. The UN fighters flew with bombers to cut supply routes and to restrict the enemy's ability to move in daylight.

The first Soviet-built MiG aircraft (below) to appear in the Korean sky were a shock to the UN forces. Initially flown by Soviet and Chinese pilots, these fighters were operated in greater numbers than UN planes and proved to be more than a match for the UN aircraft, most of which were older and propeller-driven.

MiG-15

PEACE OR TRUCE?

By 1953 both sides had established themselves virtually where they had started three years earlier. Long peace negotiations were conducted and although the fighting stopped, both sides of the 38th Parallel remained armed camps. North and South Korea are still technically at war, but there has been a 50-year truce.

THE COLD WAR

After the Second World War the Western Allies became increasingly concerned by the Soviet domination of Eastern Europe. In 1946 British Prime Minister Winston Churchill warned of an 'iron curtain' cutting through the middle of Europe. The Soviet leader Joseph Stalin felt that the war had been the result of "capitalist imperialism" and that war might re-occur. This mistrust led to the 'Cold War' period which involved hostility between the two power blocks, the USA and USSR on opposing sides. This led to an arms race, especially in nuclear weapons. Some actual wars were fought in the Far East where Communist influence was spreading.

East German border guards on the Berlin Wall

THE BERLIN WALL

At the end of the Second World War, Germany was split into two parts, West Germany and East Germany. Berlin was in the Soviet-dominated zone of East Germany and the city itself was similarly divided into zones. In 1961, the Soviets began constructing a wall (left), covered with barbed wire and surrounded by minefields, to divide Berlin into two zones and prevent Germans from escaping from the Communist-governed East to the West. The Berlin Wall stood until its demolition in November 1989. In October 1990, East and West Germany were reunified.

US pilot badges from the Cold War period

Lockheed SR-71, or Blackbird, used for spy flights over enemy territory

NUCLEAR WEAPONS

In September 1949 the Soviet Union tested an atomic weapon and a period of superpower rivalry began, bringing the world to the brink of destruction. Soviet May Day celebrations in Moscow began featuring parades of missiles and in 1962 the Soviet Union placed missiles on Cuba, close to the USA. It was forced to remove them when President Kennedy blockaded Cuba but this incident became known as the Cuban Missile Crisis. A 'hot line' was installed linking the White House with the Kremlin. In 1985 Strategic Arms Limitation (SALT) negotiations were renewed and tensions reduced further with the collapse of a Soviet-dominated Eastern Europe.

SPY PLANES

Throughout the Cold War both sides used increasingly sophisticated methods of spying on each other. One incident took place in 1960 when the Soviets, who were using a new missile system, announced that they had shot down an American Lockheed U2 plane in Soviet airspace. Although the US denied he was spying, the pilot, Gary Powers, was held captive before eventually being released. Later aircraft used 'stealth technology' to remain undetected by radar. Many of these missions were eventually carried out by satellites – a spin-off from the 'Space Race' of the 1960s and 1970s.

Soviet missiles being paraded during the Cuban Missile Crisis, Havana 1963

VIETNAM, 1965-72

Vietnam was occupied by the Japanese in the Second World War but in 1945 the French attempted to regain control of what had been their colony. The Viet Minh, a communist-inspired resistance movement, had other ideas about who should govern the country. Vietnam descended into a guerrilla war and the French were beaten in May 1954 at Dien Bien Phu. Although a pro-western government was installed in the south of Vietnam it was obvious that unless a final peace could be achieved the communists would gain control. The United States sent advisors and used air power to support southern Vietnam and by 1965 they deployed combat troops as well. The US was gradually drawn into an escalating struggle in which more men and resources were required in the search for victory.

Map of South East Asia at the time of the Vietnam conflict

HELICOPTERS

The US believed that the use of helicopter 'air cavalry' would provide flexibile transportation for troops and wounded and would help to solve the problem of locating guerrilla fighters. During the war 4,857 helicopters were lost. Helicopters gave the US forces advantages, but they alone could not win the war.

Bell Huey US helicopter

HO CHI MINH

As a revolutionary leader, Hoi Chi Minh provided inspiration to the tens of thousands of men, women and children who resisted the Americans and fought for the North Vietnamese forces. His words were even played on the radio and 'Uncle Ho' believed his inspiration would help the people to drive out the foreigners.

GUERRILLA WARFARE

The North Vietnamese fighters blended in with the civilian population, used tunnel systems to hide and could strike at vulnerable targets before moving into remote areas where they were difficult to identify. US bombing raids and the use of defoliants, to kill off the jungle, and napalm did little to hamper their enemies although tens of thousands of civilians died or were injured. From 1972 the United States withdrew ground troops from Vietnam and in April 1975 the last Americans evacuated Saigon as the communist army flooded into South Vietnam and captured the capital.

North Vietnamese guerrilla fighters

HOSTILE ENVIRONMENT

Once on the ground the US Army had to deal with a hostile environment – paddy fields, jungle, 'booby traps' and an enemy who was a master of camouflage.

Nowhere was safe and men waited for their 12-month tour of duty to end so they could go home.

GULF WAR, 1991

Middle East

On 2nd August, 1990, Iraqi President Saddam Hussein ordered the invasion of the small, oil-rich state of Kuwait. The invasion was condemned by the United Nations and they passed resolutions to use all necessary means to free Kuwait. The war that followed, from 16th January to 28th February, 1991, was fought by a coalition of countries including the USA, Britain, France and a number of European and Middle Eastern countries. Kuwait and Saudi Arabia provided financial backing. Well before the first bombs were dropped US agents inserted a 'virus' into Iraq's military computers disabling much of the country's air defence system. The war began with a series of air strikes on targets including airfields, control systems and power stations. Later targets were units of the army and before the land war – 'Operation Desert Storm' – started many Iraq units were unable to fight.

M-1A1 ABRAMS
This battle tank used by coalition forces had a 105-mm calibre gun, plus three machine guns. It weighed 63 tonnes, but still managed a maximum speed of 72 kph. During the land battle hundreds of Iraqi armoured vehicles were destroyed with a minimum loss of coalition forces.

F-117a
Stealth Fighter

F-117A STEALTH FIGHTER
This was the first war in which the Stealth Fighter participated. The aircraft was so secret that it was in service for six years before the US Air Force admitted it existed. The fighter was able to approach an enemy without being detected. In the Gulf War it was used as a bomber because accuracy was vitally important.

M-1A1 Abrams

SCUD MISSILES

The Iraqi army in Kuwait was well equipped and experienced, having just fought a successful eight-year war against Iran. Iraqi Scud missiles had the range and accuracy to hit a coalition base in Saudi Arabia or even targets in Israel. They could also carry explosives or chemical warheads. To meet this threat, coalition aircraft sought out the Scud launching units, while special forces, including the British Special Air Service (SAS) were sent deep into Iraq to detect the launch sites. These forces used a variety of vehicles including the Humvee and British Light Strike Vehicle. More than 80 Scuds were fired and a new US anti-missile system, the 'Patriot', was deployed for the first time to destroy them in flight.

AH-64 Apache

*Coalition forces'
dune buggy*

*Hand-held
missile launcher*

AH-64 APACHE

The Apache (top right) acted as the American army's main anti-armour helicopter and carried Hellfire missiles with a range of 6 km.

*Soldier of the US
Airborne Divison*

AIRBORNE TROOPS

One feature of the war was the use of airborne troops to establish advanced bases inside Iraq. This was to cut off Iraqi forces and help the attack which was aimed at cutting off the main road linking Kuwait with Basra in Iraq.

HAND-HELD MISSILES

The US Stinger missile system could bring down enemy aircraft and was sent to the conflict in the Gulf. However, it had little use due to the almost complete destruction of the Iraqi air force on the ground.

TIMESPAN

1899-1902
The Boer War is fought in South Africa. It is the first guerrilla war of the 20th century.

1901
The British monarch, Queen Victoria, dies.

1903
Orville and Wilbur Wright conduct the first powered flight in the USA. Nations across the world start to develop the first air forces.

1904-1905
The Russo-Japanese War involves the siege of Port Arthur in Manchuria and leads to the defeat of the Russian fleet at Tsushima.

1914
The assassination of the heir to the Austro-Hungarian throne, Archduke Franz Ferdinand, results in the Great War (later to be known as the First World War). War on the Western Front becomes a trench stalemate until August 1918.

1916
The British government introduces conscription instead of relying on volunteers for its armed forces. The minimum age for call-up is 18.

1918
On 11th November, Germany signs the Armistice and the war ends. The Treaty of Versailles punishes Germany for the conflict. People continue to die all over the world due to the influenza epidemic. The 'flu' eventually kills over 21 million people, more than the war.

1919
John Alcock and Arthur Brown complete the first non-stop flight across the Atlantic and land in Ireland. World air travel is now possible.

1933
Adolf Hitler, leader of the National Socialist (Nazi) party becomes Chancellor of Germany and begins to re-arm the nation.

1936-1938
Civil War in Spain brings the fascist leader General Franco to power.

1938
German troops occupy Czechoslovakia.

1939
Hitler orders the German invasion of Poland. Britain and France declare war on Nazi Germany.

Iron Cross, service medal awarded to German soldiers in the Second World War

1940
German forces occupy France. Only the RAF can prevent an invasion of Britain. The Battle of Britain is fought between July and September.

June 1941
Nazi Germany invades the USSR. Britain has an ally.

December 1941
Japanese forces attack the US Pacific fleet in Pearl Harbor, Hawaii. The USA declares war on both Japan and Nazi Germany.

May 1944
Berlin falls to the Soviet army on 2nd May and the German army surrenders two days later – Victory in Europe Day.

June 1944
Britain and the USA land in occupied France. The 'second front' opens.

Tank from the Great War

US transport aircraft, Douglas DC-4

August 1945
Following two atomic bombs Japan surrenders. Fourteenth August is VJ (Victory in Japan) Day.

1946
The Cold War begins with the creation of an 'Iron Curtain' between the USSR, its satellite countries and the West.

1948
Soviet leader Joseph Stalin blockades road and rail routes to West Berlin to starve its population or force them into Soviet control. The US organises airlifts to the city for 328 days, landing an average of 7,000 tonnes of supplies per day. The blockade is called off in May 1949.

1950
The Soviet-trained Korean People's Army attacks US-held Southern Korea, starting the Korean War. The conflict involves forces from North Korea, the USSR, China and the United Nations.

1953
North and South Korea form a truce and fighting stops. The Korean War claimed the lives of more than two million people.

1965
Tensions escalate in Vietnam and the US becomes involved in a guerrilla war against North Vietnamese communist fighters.

1972
Defeated, the last US ground forces withdraw from Vietnam.

1975
The US embassy in Saigon is evacuated as the North Vietnamese take control of the capital of South Vietnam. The city is renamed Ho Chi Minh City.

North Vietnamese guerrilla fighters

1978
The Soviet Union invades Afghanistan to impose a communist government. Muslim rebels fight a long, drawn-out guerrilla war from the mountains.

1982
Argentina invades the Falkland Islands in the South Atlantic, which lie approximately 500 km from the Argentinian coast but are ruled by Great Britain. Britain sends a task force over 8,000 km to recapture the territory.

1991
The First Gulf War occurs. Iraq invades neighbouring Kuwait and a UN-backed coalition defeats Iraqi forces and recaptures the state.

1992
Soviet troops are eventually pushed out of Afghanistan.

1994
Following the collapse of Yugoslavia, the various ethnic and religious groups that make up the population fight a complex war in which thousands of civilians are killed. UN and NATO (North Atlantic Treaty Organisation) troops are sent to Bosnia and Kosovo.

GLOSSARY

Aces Pilots who have shot down more than ten enemy aircraft.

Armistice An agreement between armies to suspend a conflict and discuss terms of peace.

Artillery A term to describe guns, mortars and missile launchers larger than those carried by a soldier.

Atomic bomb A weapon using nuclear fission to cause an explosion with massive destructive power.

Banzai charge An attack made by Japanese troops with bayonets and swords.

Blitzkrieg 'Lightning War', a description of the fast, mobile and mechanised German attacks first used against Poland in 1939.

Bolsheviks The early Russian communist party.

Booby trap An explosive weapon designed to kill or injure an unsuspecting soldier.

Bully beef Preserved meat in tins, a basic food ration for British soldiers in the early 20th century.

Calibre The term used to describe the diameter of an artillery barrel.

Central Powers The alliance between Germany and Austro-Hungary.

Concentration camps Originally used as protection for civilians, but under the Nazi regime they came to be death camps.

Conscription Enforced recruitment into the armed forces.

Convoy The system in which merchant ships were gathered together to make voyages under the protection of warships.

Dogfight Aerial combat between two or more aircraft.

Empire A collection of peoples and territories under the rule of a single person or state.

Fascist A term originally used to describe a supporter of the Italian dictator Benito Mussolini, later for any right wing movement.

Führer German word for 'leader' and the title Adolf Hitler gave himself as the ruler of Germany.

Guerrilla war A war fought in a secret or underhand way.

Gurkhas Soldiers from Nepal who have fought for Britain since the early 19th century.

Infantry Soldiers who fight on foot with hand-held weapons.

Iron curtain A term used by British Prime Minister Winston Churchill to describe the division of Europe between the Soviet Union and Western powers.

Ironclad A wooden warship with iron or steel armour plating.

Khaki An Indian word meaning 'dusty', used to describe the colour of the British uniform.

Mobilisation Equipping and preparing an army for war.

Mulberry harbours The name given to the two floating harbours taken to Normandy by the Allies in 1944.

Napalm Jellied petrol dropped from aircraft as a weapon.

NATO The North Atlantic Treaty Organisation. An organisation of western states originally created to combat the threat from the USSR.

Nazi The National Socialist German Workers' Party which came to power in Germany in 1933.

Republic A state in which the people or their elected representatives hold power, rather than a king or queen.

Rounds Bullets or other ammunition.

Sonar Sound navigation and ranging – a detection system used to locate targets underwater.

Torpedo An explosive device driven through water by a propeller.

Trench A ditch dug by soldiers to offer protection.

USSR Union of Soviet Socialist Republics, sometimes referred to as the Soviet Union.

INDEX

Page numbers in bold refer to illustrations